JOHN TRAVOLTA

" QUOTE UNQUOTE "

JOHN TRAVOLTA

" QUOTE UNQUOTE "

Bob McCabe

**CRESCENT
BOOKS**

New York • Avenel

PICTURE ACKNOWLEDGEMENTS
London Features International: 6, 10, 13, 14, 15, 21, 23; Nick Elgar 9;
Ronald Grant Archive: front cover, 12, 16, 18, 19, 24, 25, 26, 28, 30, 31, 32, 33, 34, 35, 36,
39, 40, 41, 42, 45, 46, 48, 50, 51, 55, 56, 59, 60, 63, 64, 66, 67, 69, 70, 72, 74, 77, 78;
Retna: back cover; © Theodore Wood 73; **Alan Jones**: 53.
Every effort has been made to trace the copyright holders and we apologize in advance for any unintentional omissions.
We would be pleased to insert the appropriate acknowledgement in any subsequent edition of this publication.

This 1996 edition is published by Crescent Books,
a division of Random House Value Publishing, Inc.,
40 Engelhard Avenue, Avenel, New Jersey 07001.

Crescent Books and colophon are registered trademarks of Random House Value Publishing, Inc.

Random House
New York ● Toronto ● London ● Sydney ● Auckland

First published in th UK in 1996

Copyright © Parragon Book Service Ltd 1996

ISBN: 0-517-18446-X

8 7 6 5 4 3 2 1

A CIP catalog record for this book is available from the Library of Congress

Produced by Haldane Mason, London

Editor: Paul Barnett
Design: Zoë Mellors
Picture Research: Charles Dixon-Spain

Printed in Italy

CONTENTS

FROM ENGLEWOOD TO HOLLYWOOD 6

FEVER 26

FAR FROM PERFECT 42

LOOK WHO'S TALKING BACK! 60

THE COMEBACK KING 70

FILMOGRAPHY 80

FROM ENGLEWOOD TO HOLLYWOOD

'Like Ray Charles once said: "You better be nice to people on your way up, because you're gonna meet them on your way up again."'

FACING PAGE: *John Travolta dances the Batusi in* Pulp Fiction.

F SCOTT FITZGERALD famously wrote that there are no second acts in American lives. John Travolta has proven him wrong. The white-suited Tony Manero of *Saturday Night Fever* (1977) and the leather-jacketed Danny Zuko of *Grease* (1978) were images that helped define American cinema in the 1970s, making Travolta the biggest American superstar since Elvis Presley. But, as with Elvis, the movies didn't always know what to make of him, so in the 1980s he made a series of movies that practically destroyed what was then Hollywood's most glittering career. No actor had ever gone so far so fast in Hollywood, but, equally, few have ever shown such a lack of judgement in maintaining such a career or experienced such a fall from grace.

But in 1994 all that changed — with a little help from filmmaker Quentin Tarantino. *Pulp Fiction* became a movie phenomenon, helping to define the cinema of the 1990s in the same way *Saturday Night Fever* had the 1970s. At the centre of it all was John Travolta, reborn as a movie icon — older, wiser but, as the second Oscar nomination of his career confirmed, just as talented an actor as before.

John Travolta is the only actor in Hollywood history ever to have become a superstar in two distinctly different eras, and recently attained the distinction of becoming the highest-paid actor in Hollywood history.

Travolta family legend begins with a kidnapping. Neapolitan Salvatore Travolta swept his love Giuseppina Marsala off the deck of an ocean liner bound for her native Sicily. A traditional wedding quickly followed to save the girl's honour, and from this union five children were born, among them Salvatore Jr.

'I said, once you've become a character you are another person. You have to be quiet when it's not your turn. And you just don't make an entrance by running into a room. You let people have a look at you when you walk in.'

HELEN TRAVOLTA'S ACTING ADVICE TO HER SON JOHN

ABOVE: *John Travolta with father, Sam.*

nearby Hillsdale. His wife Helen, of Irish-American extraction, had formerly worked as an actress, appearing as one of the Sunshine Sisters on Hackensack Radio during the 1930s. In 1931 she had set a record for swimming the Hudson River. Settling down with Sam, she instantly immersed herself in local stock theatre and worked as an acting teacher.

The small middle-class suburb of Englewood, New Jersey – once described by its most famous son as 'hardly any place at all' – was a far cry from these romantic beginnings, but it was here that Salvatore 'Sam' Travolta Jr settled with his wife Helen.

Sam had played semi-professional baseball and football but, when his own family started arriving, he opened a business, the Travolta Tyre Exchange, in

'My mother and father were both 42 when I was born, so by the time I started picking up their vibes, they were already 50. I started looking at life through their eyes . . . what I observed were 50-year-old parents and their anxieties, their blues, their sensing the third chapter of their lives. That's never left me and, as a result, I have always had an older person's point of view on life. In other words I sense the end. I get blue more easily because I'm not always appreciating the youth I have.'

Sam and Helen had six children. A daughter, Ellen, was born first, followed by son Sam. Margaret, Anne and Joey followed, and then, on February 18, 1954, Helen gave birth to her final child, a son: John.

LEFT: *An early Travolta publicity shot.*

'I reckon we were all demanding kids. But I was the real cherry on the cake. It was all "I want" and "Gimme, gimme". I insisted on being the centre of attention.'

As a child John Travolta was long and lean, prompting his brother Joey to nick-name him 'Bone'. 'I'd come home from work', recalled John's father Sam, 'and Joey, who was always cracking jokes any-way, would say to me in front of Johnny, "Hey, dad, what's left of a chicken after all the meat is gone?" And I'd laugh and say, "Why, the bone." Johnny would get very upset and hurt, thinking that Joey *and* I were making fun of him.'

Despite such petty squabbles the Travoltas were a close, loving family, all

ABOVE: *Joey Travolta in Sunnyside.*

eight of them crammed into a three-bedroomed house. John grew up sharing an attic room with his two brothers. As the youngest child, he was clearly doted on by Helen. All the children had been encouraged by their mother to get involved in the performance arts but, even early on, John was the one who showed the most aptitude, and Helen continually nurtured his talent.

When John was six, his father bought him a soundtrack recording of *Gypsy,* with Ethel Merman. John instantly retreated to the basement, where he spent his time learning by heart all the roles on the record. When he was ready, he invited his parents downstairs to watch his one-man interpretation of the classic musical. His siblings weren't invited for fear they might ridicule him, although his sister Ellen did get to see the act later when John visited her while she was in the road company of one of the play's productions. 'He'd mouth all of Merman's songs from the record', she recalled, 'and he could dance all the songs.'

Helen wanted to do her best by the performer she clearly saw in her youngest son, so by age nine he was taking lessons at a local dance school run by Fred Kelly, who sold his services largely on the hook that he was Gene Kelly's brother. But, despite his obvious talents, John's main interest at the time seemed to lie in planes. 'He loved flight and airplanes,' his father recalled, 'involving

---

'As a kid in New Jersey I'd lie awake nights listening to DC-3s flying out of La Guardia airport — heading west. I'd think about the people in them who were going somewhere. It was very romantic to me.'

ABOVE: *Boyhood idol
James Cagney in* Yankee
Doodle Dandy.

Merman or impersonating his father smoking. His favourite subject, however, was James Cagney, in particular Cagney's performance in *Yankee Doodle Dandy* (1942), the movie in which the star for once forsook his familiar gangster image to play a song-and-dance man. John later described Cagney as 'the *only* one outside my family who was a main source of inspiration'. Helen often used this adulation to her advantage. Whenever John misbehaved during his childhood she would pretend to phone Cagney and relay the message that Cagney wanted him to do what his mother told him. Eager to believe that Cagney was actually

himself with anything connected with them.'

One summer, Sam and John decided to build a plane of their own in the back garden. It was an ambitious project, with the wings and fuselage constructed from wooden planks and automobile batteries co-opted to power the propellers. Needless to say, John was disappointed his home-made plane never actually got him off the ground.

From an early age John was an excellent mimic, whether he was doing Ethel

'I always had this ability to observe people, watch them awhile and very quickly absorb their essence and then reproduce it. Nobody told me to do that. I just always stored things up about people, and, when I had a character to create, I found I had this whole reserve of behaviour and mannerisms to draw on.'

'My mother got me in as an observer, but she didn't have to urge me. Man, nobody pushed me into show business, I was aching for it! . . . I was stunned. They would break character to talk to the director, and then instantly fall right back into character. I mean, I hadn't known they'd been acting, they were so real to me.'
ON THE ACTORS' STUDIO

RIGHT: *Travolta sings!*

taking an interest in him, John always then did what his mother asked.

When a workshop from the Actors' Studio came to New Jersey, Travolta finally found an outlet for his burgeoning talent. The famous New York-based company had in the 1950s popularized what came to be known as 'the Method', via such actors as Marlon Brando, Paul Newman and even Marilyn Monroe, who had trained there. Based on the teachings of Russian drama theorist Konstantin Stanislavsky, the Method was seen at the time as a revolutionary approach to

'Whatever new dance came to school, I learned it. I think the blacks accepted me because I cared about them accepting me. They seemed to have a better sense of humour, a looser style, I wanted to be like that.'

naturalism in performance. Helen Travolta took John along to the workshop, an event that proved to be the defining moment of his young life.

The representatives of the Actors' Studio were so impressed with John that they cast him, at age 12, in a production of *Who'll Save the Ploughboy?* Interestingly, this workshop was to be the only acting training John ever had.

In high school, John met his best friend-to-be Jerry Wurms, who would one day become the head of John's production company. But such things were not on their minds in school – and neither was school-work: both boys showed more interest in music, dancing and hanging out. 'We were both taught to dance by the blacks,' Jerry later recalled.

LEFT: John before the big breaks into TV and film.

'Somebody in the corridors or outside always had a radio, and somebody was always dancing.'

By the time he turned 16, John knew that his school career was going nowhere. After all, why should he worry about education? The Actors' Studio and his stock appearances had convinced him his future lay in acting, so he said good-bye to academia and headed across the river to New York. Helen, as always, was supportive, seeing in him a chance for the success she had never really had as an actress herself. Sam, however, was more cautious, offering his son a get-out clause – he had one year, and if by the end of that time things hadn't worked out John would come back and finish school. He never did.

'The luck came fast,' Travolta later recalled, 'but not the success.' Initially he moved in with his sister Anne, who was already in the city pursuing her own acting career. Small roles came quickly for John, although they were not often long-lived. His off-Broadway debut, for example, in a play called *Rain,* closed after just five days.

He was soon spotted, though, by manager Bob LeMond, who was greatly impressed by John's strong, dark, Italian

LEFT: *In the 1980s John had not lost any of his charm, as LeMond said in 1971, 'He was a dream.'*

looks and his piercing blue eyes. 'He was a dream,' explained LeMond, who was to remain Travolta's personal manager for over a decade. 'He got the first part I ever sent him up for, and he's never been turned down since.' As fond as he was of his protegé, LeMond was equally fond of hyperbole; Travolta in fact failed his very first film audition, losing the lead in *Panic in Needle Park* (1971) to a young actor called Al Pacino. Ironically, a few years later, in *Saturday Night Fever,* John's character Tony Manero would be mistaken on the dance-floor for Pacino – 'I just kissed Al Pacino,' said one of the girls.

The young actor was, however, a success when it came to auditioning for television advertisements, making over 40 during the next few years. Honda, h.i.s. slacks and the US Marines benefited from the early shine of Travolta's screen magic. The money from commercials was pretty good for a struggling actor, and Travolta was quick to put it to use, pursuing another childhood dream – he took flying lessons.

John's sights, however, were still firmly set on legitimate theatre. At the age of 19 he landed his biggest role to date, as Doody in the touring company of the new smash hit musical *Grease*. Two significant things happened to John on that tour. He decided he'd be old enough to play the lead role of greaser Danny Zuko when they came to make the movie version; and he met Marilu Henner, a young actress in the production's chorus. They became instant friends, but it wasn't until late into the production's eight-month run that they became romantically involved, establishing a sporadic relationship they maintained into the mid-1980s.

When the run came to an end, John and Marilu headed back to New York and moved in together. Both made their Broadway debut in the same production, *Over Here!*, in 1974. This was essentially a vehicle for former stars the Andrew Sisters, but it finally offered John a chance to sing and dance on the Great White Way. On the advice of manager Bob LeMond, John had, meanwhile, been making occasional trips to California for television work, guesting on such popular shows as *Emergency, The Rookies* and *Owen Marshall, Counsellor-at-Law.*

When he was offered the sum of $750 a week to appear in a production of *The Ritz* on Broadway, Travolta thought this was as good as life could get. Here was he, the kid from Englewood, New Jersey, with a part in a Broadway show that would earn him more money than he had ever seen before. So it took some persuading before Bob LeMond was able to convince him to turn down the play and head off to Los Angeles for keeps, in the hope of landing a role in a proposed new television comedy that focused on a group of rowdy teenagers in an inner-city classroom. Though dubious about the move, Travolta followed his agent's advice and, like countless actors before him, headed west.

Out in Los Angeles he hooked up once again with his high-school friend Jerry Wurms, regularly arriving at auditions courtesy of the back of Wurms's motorbike. He failed auditions for the movie version of *Jesus Christ Superstar* (1973) and *The Last Detail* (1973), the latter a role he desperately wanted since it would have given him a chance to work opposite Jack Nicholson.

The first movie role he did land was considerably less appealing. *The Devil's Rain* (1975) was a low-budget horror movie centred on a modern coven of witches; it starred Ernest Borgnine, Ida Lupino and William Shatner. John arrived on location in Durango, Mexico,

LEFT: *Despite the foolishness of* The Devil's Rain *in 1975 John has still managed to attain the heights of the BAFTA awards twenty years later.*

by all accounts depressed at the prospect of having given up Broadway for this shoestring production. As it was, his role in the final movie consists of delivering the embarrassing line – 'Blasphemer! Get him, he is a blasphemer!'

However, something far more significant was to happen to John in Durango. Joan Prather, a young actress who was likewise listed low down the movie's cast list, introduced John to the work of the Church of Scientology.

Founded by science-fiction novelist L. Ron Hubbard in the 1950s, Scientology can loosely be described as a system of self-help beliefs, many based around the idea of 'auditing', a form of therapy in which actions, emotions and their effects are gauged by a device called an E-meter. Its advocates – Travolta, Tom Cruise and Priscilla and Lisa Marie Presley among them – have publicly supported this latter-day form of religion, while its detractors have often presented the group as a glorified cult that is determined to increase its public profile by attracting celebrities to the fold, pointing to the 'church's' Hollywood-based Celebrity Centre (where Travolta maintains a fourth-floor apartment) as a prime example of this.

Despite the often controversial nature of the 'church' and its teachings, it has ever since remained a constant in Travolta's life, and he is still probably its most public member, often citing in interviews the ways it has helped his personal life and career.

It was in 1975, after completing *The Devil's Rain,* that John Travolta had another experience that would change his life forever. The television show his manager, Bob LeMond, had originally sent

---

'I've always hurt inside. I had a roller-coaster kind of happiness – up, down, up, down again. I did try analysis, it wasn't for me. But Scientology – it was like something I could use to discover myself. A means of self-help. A meter shows you when your body's responding to a bad memory you call up. You can really examine hidden pain that way, define it, put it in its place. It seemed to me very logical.'

---

him out to Los Angeles to test for, now called *Welcome Back Kotter,* was soon to go on air . . . and John had landed the role of Vinnie Barbarino. Originally conceived as a vehicle for comic Gabe Kaplan, *Welcome Back Kotter* focused on a Brooklyn-born teacher who returned to his old high school to take on a group of difficult remedial pupils. These so-called 'Sweathogs' were the outcasts of the school system; Vinnie Barbarino was their none-too-bright leader.

The show debuted on American television in September 1975 and within just a few weeks it was clear that Kaplan wasn't its only star.

The 1970s were the glory days for America's three television networks. Video and cable were yet to challenge their dominance, and sitcoms in particular – from *Happy Days* to *Three's Company* to *Laverne and Shirley* – were proving hugely popular with audiences, and were also cheap to make. Travolta's arresting good looks and stunning blue eyes leapt, as it were, out of the television screen and on to the pages of the prodigious teen pin-up magazines. Within a few weeks he was receiving no fewer than 10,000 fan letters a week, and the scripts of *Welcome Back Kotter* were being rewrit-

> *'I used to feel a little guilty about owning two planes. Then, one day, I had a long talk with myself. I said, "Hell, John, you're allowed to change with your success. Your fans want you to change." So instead of a house I bought an aeroplane.'*

ten in order to give audiences more of what they wanted – teen heart-throb Vinnie Barbarino.

Exactly the same thing had happened two years before to television's other leading pin-up, the Fonz. Henry Winkler began *Happy Days* as one of the many supporting players to the more established Ron Howard, but rapidly became the star of the show as audiences responded to his character. Now John was enjoying the same effect. A television sitcom had made him a star.

It also led to a sizable increase in his bank balance, and John was quick to put his money to good use: he bought himself a plane – a DC-3 to be precise,

just like the ones he had used to listen to taking off at night back home in New Jersey. As yet more money came rolling in he added to his collection with a single-engine Air Coupe, spending his weekends away from *Kotter* flying and tending his aircraft.

Keen to exploit John's teen appeal, Midsong Records offered him a contract. His first album, released in 1976 and titled simply *John Travolta*, featured a collection of safe, middle-of-the-road songs, all sung in a pleasant enough though not particularly strong voice. Nevertheless, John's television success soon guaranteed him a place in the record charts, and 'Let Her In' became a hit single. Later that year he picked up the Billboard Award for Best New Pop Male Vocalist of the Year, and he performed at the awards ceremony, televised on CBS. A second album, *Can't Let You Go*, was rushed out the same year. This consisted of more of the same sort of MOR-style songs, mixed in with some standards. It too spawned a hit single, 'Slow Dancing'.

The Devil's Rain had been a lacklustre debut. When Travolta once again found himself in front of a movie camera,

ABOVE: *Travolta with Carrie co-star Nancy Allen.*

playing a supporting role in Brian DePalma's *Carrie* (1976), he was in a different league. DePalma was already a well-respected movie director; this was to be his first major blockbuster. Based on the novel by Stephen King, first published in 1974, this told of a shy high-school girl (played by Sissy Spacek) possessed of telekinetic powers who was abused at home by an unbalanced fundamentalist-Christian mother and ridiculed at school for her sexual backwardness and (perceived) ugliness. Travolta played one of the tormentors whose efforts precipitated the spectacularly blood-drenched finale in which Carrie takes revenge on all the bullies. He may not have had a lead role, but he was prominently featured and, more importantly, was working with a first-class director like DePalma and a first-class cast which included Spacek, Amy Irving and Piper Laurie. DePalma and Travolta formed a strong friendship, and five years later would work together again, on *Blow Out* (1981), with Travolta this time in the lead and giving one of his very best performances.

During his summer break from *Welcome Back Kotter*, Midsong Records wanted John to go on a promotional tour. 'The money to do this would have been tremendous,' he later admitted. 'Like, $25,000 per appearance, the total was up in six figures. Just to sign autographs.' But, despite all these potential riches, he put art ahead of commerce and opted for a tour in the play *Bus Stop*.

In *Kotter*, Travolta had managed to imbue the character of Vinnie Barbarino with a great deal more depth than the script had originally suggested. He had taken a one-dimensional Italian dimwit and fashioned a kid who was both vulnerable and funny, smarter than expected and certainly more likable. But still — as with all

the other characters in the show – the sitcom format kept him perilously close to being one-dimensional.

After a year of being America's number one poster boy for pre-pubescents, *Carrie* and *Bus Stop* had reminded him of the challenge of acting, and now he wanted to capitalize on that, both for himself and for his career. His next move had to be something that would give him room to grow as a performer and in the minds of his now sizable audience.

The Boy in the Plastic Bubble (1976), a made-for-television movie, was based on the true story of a boy born without any immune system. Travolta played Todd, the teenager who'd spent all his life

'I wanted to act, and the guy in the play's this very naive cowboy; it was a chance to fight that typing thing. The record-promotion people just wanted to go with the heat of the moment, with the Vinnie Barbarino fame. They weren't interested in my skills or talents. And I care about product, not PR.'

ABOVE: *John's star set in the pavement on Hollywood Boulevarde.*

inside a hermetically sealed environment. The movie was directed by Randal Kleiser, who just two years later would direct John in *Grease*. It co-starred Robert Reed, best known as Mike Brady in the popular sitcom *The Brady Bunch,* and Diana Hyland, an acclaimed stage actress who had spent some time on the quintessential 1960s soap *Peyton Place.* Over its closing credits the movie featured the song 'What Would They Say' from John's second album.

The Boy in the Plastic Bubble represented a significant breakthrough for Travolta on screen, but his off-screen life during its making was even more eventful. Although Diana Hyland was 18 years his senior and was cast as his mother, she and John fell completely in love and quickly became an inseparable couple, with Travolta also establishing an instant and sincere rapport with Diana's six-year-old son Zachary.

At the age of 22, John Travolta was one of the biggest names on television. Only one thing remained: movie stardom. Just a few days after *The Boy in the Plastic Bubble* finished filming, producer Robert Stigwood held a major press conference to announce to the media of the world that this was not far away.

'I don't think people thought I'd be as convincing in it as I ultimately was. I think they cast me because I was in a hit series on television and they figured they'd get a good rating if they used me. I really think I surprised them with my interpretation of that character.'
ON *THE BOY IN THE PLASTIC BUBBLE*

RIGHT: *John's fellow actor in* The Boy In The Plastic Bubble, *Diana Hyland — they were also lovers.*

FEVER

'No one can fully define star quality, but you can find illustration enough. And in 1978 that walk is the best one around.'
TIME MAGAZINE ON TRAVOLTA IN
SATURDAY NIGHT FEVER

FACING PAGE: *Travolta and Karen Lynn Gorney take to the dance floor in* Saturday Night Fever.

IN 1976 ROBERT STIGWOOD signed Travolta to a three-picture deal for the then princely sum of $1 million. Along with his partner Allan Carr, Stigwood had purchased the movie rights to the hit musical *Grease* and planned to cast John in the lead role, Danny Zuko. However, in order to maximize the show's stage profits, a clause in the deal stipulated that a movie version could not be released until 1978. While they waited, Stigwood and Carr had to find another vehicle for the man they had decided would be their ascendant star.

And Travolta's star was certainly ascending. On November 12 *The Boy in the Plastic Bubble* was aired to high ratings and critical acclaim, much of it focusing on the strength of Travolta's moving performance. A week later, *Carrie* opened, rapidly becoming a sizable hit with audiences and critics alike.

John's romance with Diana Hyland was also going from strength to strength, but, unsure of how the age difference would be accepted, they had so far kept things under wraps. On December 19 they decided to go public, and Diana accompanied John to the Golden Apple Awards ceremony; these awards are presented yearly by the Hollywood

LEFT: *Travolta as Tony Manero in* Saturday Night Fever.

Women's Press Club. John had been nominated in the Best New Star of the Year category. He failed to get the award, but he stole the evening's thunder as the paparazzi clamoured to get a picture of Travolta and his older woman.

Robert Stigwood sent Travolta a script called *Saturday Night Fever,* which he saw as a possible stopgap movie before *Grease* could begin filming. Based on a *New York* magazine article, 'Tribal Rites of Saturday Night' by journalist Nik Cohn, *Saturday Night Fever* told the story of Tony Manero, a young Brooklyn kid who escapes his boring life and repressive family by dancing the night away at the local disco, coming alive on the dance-floor, the only place where his life makes sense to him. Peppered with strong language, the script (written by Norman Wexler) managed perfectly to capture the sights and sensations of a burgeoning strand of youth culture as well as the depressing realities of the lives of young Brooklynites ensnared in this trap.

Travolta was unsure of the project at first. 'Even when I saw all of Tony's levels,' he explained, 'he still didn't seem to me a sympathetic character. He's really mean to women, you know?

'She said, "Baby, you're going to be great in this." I dumbly asked why. "Baby, he's got all the colours, he's miles from what you've played. He's furious because he feels the excitement of the whole world when he dances. Staying in Brooklyn is torture for him. Catholicism has mixed this boy up; he tries on his brother's priest collar in front of the mirror — what a moment for an actor. And he grows, he gets out of Brooklyn. OK, maybe all that isn't in the script, but you'll know how to put it there." I said, "Diana, he's also the king of the disco. I'm not that good a dancer." She said, "Baby, you'll learn." It was like an order. The next day I began three months of intensive disco-dance training.'

RECALLING DIANA HYLAND'S ADVICE CONCERNING HIS ROLE IN *SATURDAY NIGHT FEVER*

RIGHT: *Travolta and Gorney prepare for Saturday night.*

'I'd go in a side entrance to a table in the back, in the shadows, and it would be an hour before anybody caught sight of me. During those 60 minutes, I concentrated like hell on every bit of those kids' behaviour that I could absorb — how they talked to each other, little chance movements that were habit. The way they acted in the Odyssey was formalized. It was a ritual, with rules . . . Tony Manero's whole male-chauvinist thing, I got it from watching those guys in the disco.'

He's so angry.' Diana, however, saw in the script the perfect role for John, and convinced him to do the movie. For three months before filming began, he danced three hours a night, five days a week. In addition, he hired ex-boxer Jimmy Gambina — Sylvester Stallone's trainer for *Rocky* (1976) — to get him into shape, and over an intensive eight-week period Gambina helped John drop 10kg (22lb) in weight. John also made trips out to Brooklyn to explore life at the 2001 Odyssey club, the focus of Cohn's original article and the location at which the movie was largely to be shot.

When filming began, it quickly became clear to director John Badham that he had something special on his hands with John. 'It was very exciting to watch the rushes and realize that we had a huge new star on our hands. His magnetism amazed me.'

While John was filming *Saturday Night Fever* in Brooklyn Diana Hyland remained in California, having recently landed a role in the new television show *Eight is Enough*. But she fell ill and was forced to absent herself from the show, telling her colleagues she was suffering from a recurrent back problem. A few years earlier, she had been diagnosed as having breast cancer. Now the cancer had returned, this time in her spine, and was inoperable. When John realized just how serious her illness was he flew back to be with her. On March 27, hours after John's arrival back in Los Angeles, Diana Hyland died in his arms.

John and Diana had planned a trip to Rio later in the year. At her memorial service, he wore the white suit she had picked out for him for the holiday. When Diana won a posthumous Emmy for her performance in *The Boy in the Plastic Bubble*, John collected the award on her behalf, held it up to heaven, and said, 'Here's to you Diana, wherever you are.'

Within a few days of Diana's passing, Travolta flew back to New York to finish filming *Saturday Night Fever*. His sister

LEFT: *That paint can, that walk . . .*

'In Brooklyn we had real trouble shooting the movie, because the crowds John drew were huge, but he couldn't have been on less of a star trip. Getting the movie right obsessed him. His head was always buried in the script, and he came to see every one of the rushes — some stars don't bother . . . Of course, he did know that the movie could be his biggest shot.'

JOHN BADHAM

'When Diana was dying, she smiled and said, "You're going to carry on what I can't, baby. You're going to act like nobody else of your generation. Now remember that, baby." '

Anne had a small role in the film, as the pizza waitress, and John had particularly asked that his mother also be given a small role, as his 'thank you' to her for having got him this far; she played a paint-shop customer.

Saturday Night Fever opened in December 1977 and became nothing short of a phenomenon. The combination of the Bee Gees' music, Badham's tough, gritty vision and Travolta's sensational performance turned the movie into a smash hit that eventually earned more than $350 million at the box office (with continuing revenues from television, videos and revivals). The popularity of discos and disco music exploded, the polyester white suit (as worn by Tony Manero) became a fashion classic, dance-schools eagerly taught everyone the Hustle, and at Vidal Sassoon's hairdressing salons a special Travolta haircut was on offer for $25.

From the second that Travolta first made his appearance in *Saturday Night Fever,* strutting down the street, swinging his hips even more than he was swinging the paint can he was carrying, it was clear that a new star had arrived. Young audiences could relate to this character, who carefully combed his hair

LEFT: *Tony Manero crosses the bridge in* Saturday Night Fever.

RIGHT: Saturday Night Fever *director John Badham.*

'The pain was on every inch of his body. But John didn't want people to feel sorry for him. He knew the best thing was to plunge completely into what he was doing. Some of the best scenes in the picture were done in that advanced stage of grief.'

JOHN BADHAM

while dreaming of the night to come on the dance-floor, who worked in a dead-end job in order to afford that special shirt he just *had* to have. So much of the 1970s had been spent recovering from the fallout of the 1960s, but now *Saturday Night Fever* gave the decade a defining image all its own, chronicling and helping to create the disco culture, and offering up an icon to be worshipped the world over.

Newsweek noted how 'thousands of shaggy-haired, blue-jean-clad youngsters are suddenly putting on suits and vests, combing their hair and learning to dance with partners', and went on to quote Washington-based rock promoter Jack

Alix: 'It's the most phenomenal thing since the Beatles.'

As 'Night Fever' and 'Staying Alive' took control of the singles charts, the movie's soundtrack album went on to become the biggest-selling album of all time (a distinction it retained until the mid-1980s, when it was overtaken by Michael Jackson's *Thriller*). To mark this seismic movement in youth culture, *Time* magazine put Travolta on its cover, hailing him as a new star in the league of De Niro, Pacino and Hoffman.

The critics were equally quick to praise the movie, and in particular its star. The National Board of Review named Travolta Best Actor of the Year,

'*John is the perfect star for the Seventies. He has this strange, androgynous quality, this all-pervasive sexuality. Men don't find him terribly threatening. And women . . .*'
SATURDAY NIGHT LIVE PRODUCER
LORNE MICHAELS ON TRAVOLTA'S APPEAL

and in February 1978 John learned he had been nominated for an Academy Award. 'Just the nomination, man, I didn't come down for days. It's a great seal of approval on your acting, man. I love the Oscar.'

Fever spread to Britain on March 22, 1978, when the movie once again opened to strong reviews and record-breaking box office, despite the fact that it was awarded an X certificate (over-18s only) – ensuring that the thousands of adolescent fans who had waited months for

LEFT: Saturday Night Fever *Bee Gees*.

'It was all so amazing. The excessiveness of it all. The weird thing is I thought SATURDAY NIGHT FEVER was just going to be a stepping stone. We did the movie thinking it would be a small art film.'

their first glimpse of the Travolta magic were denied the pleasure. (In response, John Badham later re-edited the film so audiences of all ages could see it. 'I cut out every "goddamn", "son-of-a-bitch" and "hell",' he joked, but he also cut out the heart of the movie, shifting too much of the emphasis to the dance sequences and away from Tony's struggle to escape his treadmill life.)

John presented the Best Supporting Actress Award (to Vanessa Redgrave) at that year's Oscars, but failed to go home the possessor of a statuette himself. By now he was busy filming *Grease*, the movie he had prophetically hoped for when touring in the play years before. Still racked with grief over the death of Diana Hyland, he as always turned to

Scientology for help, but still nothing could change the fact that he was experiencing all this success without her there to share it with him. The filming went smoothly, with studio expectations high that the movie would allow Travolta to capture a younger audience than that for *Saturday Night Fever*.

John himself, meanwhile, decided a change of scene was what was needed.

BELOW: *Tony combs his hair for Saturday night.*

'He was pretty young and he'd had a personal tragedy and he was shell-shocked. He was a very nice man and I remember I liked him very much but he was kind of in a spin-cycle a bit.'
STOCKARD CHANNING ON FILMING *GREASE*

He left the West Hollywood penthouse he had been sharing – at various times – with Jerry Wurms, *Fever* co-star Donna Pescow, and his increasingly large collection of hand-built model airplane kits and bought a $1 million 7-hectare (17-acre) ranch in Santa Barbara. This Spanish-style home, El Adobe Tajiguas, was the perfect locale for him to indulge his increasingly opulent lifestyle – complete with a staff of servants, a pool, a pond, a tennis court and a cinema, not to mention a vintage

Thunderbird, a Mercedes, a Jaguar and, of course, a Rolls Royce in the garage, plus space to land the plane nearby.

In many ways John felt he had bought this house for his mother, to show her that all her hopes for him had paid off, all their shared dreams had come true. Helen lived there for two weeks before she too died of cancer, just eight months after Diana Hyland.

John had become a superstar in a way that most of his contemporaries would never experience. He was the first and probably the only genuine movie star the 1970s produced, and as such he found himself in an unusual situation. In 1977 *Star Wars* changed the face of movies forever, rapidly becoming the biggest money-maker of all time and heralding a fresh era of the blockbuster. In the years that followed, up-and-coming agents might become as famous as the up-and-coming talent they handled, deals would

---

'You know how sometimes you sense things on an unconscious level? You do things and you don't know exactly why. For instance, a single man doesn't have to buy a house way out in a place like Santa Barbara with a staff of people to look after things. But maybe, on another level, I knew my mother was going to pass away, and I had to do it all very fast in order to make her dream come true . . .

Maybe my being a superstar allowed my mother, who was an aspiring actress, to have that kind of lifestyle, even vicariously, before she left me . . . It was worth buying the house just for those two weeks.'

'It was fun, on one level. Nowhere near as complicated as SATURDAY NIGHT FEVER, but it still wasn't easy because I'd never played a Fifties dude on the screen before . . .
I felt that I had to think a lot about how a guy's behaviour would have differed 25 years or so before I was born.
I mean, movement had to be different. There hadn't been the drug thing, or the awareness of blacks, so none of those styles of moving or talking had happened yet.'
ON DANNY ZUKO

---

be packaged and Hollywood would see in a new age with new rules. By a curious trick of timing, Travolta's fame managed slightly to pre-date this shift in movie-making. He didn't have the luxury of a Harrison Ford or a Tom Cruise, both of whom could carefully judge and develop projects, amassing power through box-office guarantees. Travolta, by contrast, had as his reference the days of the Hollywood contract players – actors who worked because it was expected of them, actors who would go from one movie to the next on the basis that, if this one didn't work, the next one most probably would. Or the next. This mentality seriously damaged Travolta's career in the 1980s and saw him eclipsed by a generation of new leading men. As he later recalled, 'I even had other famous people come up to me and say, "John, we've learned from your mistake." And I would say, "Which one?"'

Travolta, then, found himself more aligned with the old guard of Hollywood, in particular his boyhood idol Jimmy Cagney, whom he invited to his ranch for tea. Cagney accepted, and ended up staying for three days. During that period the two men talked and watched movies, Cagney recounting stories as Travolta listened attentively. 'I gained a lot of strength from those three days with Cagney,' Travolta later admitted, delightedly. 'It taught me that a man can take a knock and still hang in there. Also, that talent and personality don't always have to wither with age.' They remained close friends until Cagney's death in 1986.

But these difficulties were ahead of him. At the time, though it was hard for John to imagine being in a movie that could top the impact of *Saturday Night Fever, Grease,* released that same year (1978), did just that. A younger audience, who had been clamouring for a glimpse of this 1970s screen legend, finally got to see Travolta on the big screen. Even before the movie's release, singles from its soundtrack were already topping the charts. Travolta's two duets with co-star Olivia Newton-John, 'You're The One That I Want' and 'Summer Nights', were global smashes; the movie rapidly followed along the same trail, proving enormously popular – nowhere more so than in London, where Travolta, attending the British premiere with Marilu Henner, was mobbed by more than 6000 fans. Legend has it that a Travolta lookalike was sent out to test the crowd's reaction, and barely made it back in one piece.

Grease went on to earn over $400 million, eclipsing *Saturday Night Fever* becoming the most successful movie musical of all time. In the space of three years and two movies, John Travolta had become the biggest star the world had seen since Elvis Presley. With two of the biggest blockbusters in cinema history, a

RIGHT: *Dancing again – Travolta and Olivia Newton-John in* Grease.

*'Start with one thing: they need you.
Without you they have an empty screen.
So when you get on there, just do
what you think is right.
. . . If you listen to all the clowns around,
you're just dead.'*
JAMES CAGNEY'S ADVICE TO
JOHN TRAVOLTA

top television show and a string of hit records to his name, John Travolta was touted as the definitive star of the 1970s. Still riding high on the success of *Grease,* he was invited to dine with President Jimmy Carter and family (daughter Amy was a big fan) at the White House, was named Male Star of the Year by the Hollywood Women's Press Club — and was even denounced in East Germany as a dreaded symbol of capitalism, the state-run newspaper *Junge Welt* claiming that 'Travolta tries to make capitalistic daily life seem harmless'. He could most prob-

LEFT: *Greased Lightning!*

RIGHT: *John Travolta, not quite stranded at the drive-in.*

ably have made any movie he wanted next; indeed he had three lined up to choose from – *American Gigolo, Moment by Moment* and *The Godfather Part 3*.

It would not be the only time in his career that Travolta made the wrong choice, but this was the most devastating.

'I had this frightening experience at the GREASE opening in London when I thought the roof of the car was going to cave in under the crush. I genuinely thought my life was about to end. It was panic point for me. And yet it was exciting too. Part of me was loving it.'

FAR FROM PERFECT

'Being a child of the Sixties and a Seventies
teenager made me understand my own
generation, even though I was probably more
career-oriented than most. But it was really
through my performances that I became
an archetype. Everyone could identify with me
because they had a friend either like me
or like one of the characters I played.
I had one quality of someone that everyone
knew in the Seventies.'

FACING PAGE: *A moment away from disaster . . .*

WITH HINDSIGHT, it's easy to blame his bad judgement in making *Moment by Moment* (1978) in some part on the double bereavement he had recently experienced. But, truth be told, it was a project that Travolta felt passionate about, and had helped to initiate. Two years earlier, he had seen comic actress Lily Tomlin's one-woman show on Broadway. 'I asked Robert Stigwood to see if Lily would be interested in doing a film,' recalled Travolta. 'Luckily, she liked some footage of me in *Fever* and agreed.' The movie concerned a young beach bum, named Strip, who fell in love with Trisha Rawlings, a Beverly Hills matron. The plot led many to view the story as a reflection of John's relationship with Diana Hyland, something he was quick to dismiss. 'In my relationship with Diana there was really no significance put on years. She just happened to be older. The movie relationship was so unlike my relationship with her.'

In many ways, Travolta viewed *Moment by Moment* as a movie that would capture the spirit of the day in the way that *Saturday Night Fever* had. He saw the role of Strip as a timely one that a young audience could relate to, with the movie dealing with issues about relationships that hadn't really been addressed in a post-1960s permissive society. He also saw it as a further opportunity to develop his range, playing a character who was very different from both Tony Manero and Danny Zuko.

If only some of these hopes and ambitions had surfaced in Jane Wagner's inane and ultimately pretentious script. Wagner was Tomlin's regular writer, but this was her first screenplay. To stack the odds even higher against the movie, Wagner was also hired as director — another 'first' for her. The movie received an R rating and hit theatres the same weekend as the biggest movie of the year, *Superman* (1978), which was a PG.

'I was in a canoe, going up this little ravine, and a native approached me and said, "John Travolta!" I said to myself, "It's over! There's no place in the world I can go . . ."'

ON TRYING TO GET AWAY FROM IT ALL IN TAHITI, 1978

RIGHT: *Travolta, with Moment by Moment co-star Lily Tomlin.*

'*I have a great affinity for the character I play and I had actually met several young men like this character. Young people nowadays take everything very seriously, according to my observations. I even notice that with fans who come up to me; everything seems important, including things that are in a lighter vein. Therefore, I think that youth will identify with the character and the emotions in this film.*'
ON *MOMENT BY MOMENT*

Even without such problems, the critical response would have been enough to ensure that *Moment by Moment* was a spectacular failure. It was as if Travolta — who had shown such promise and reached such heights — had personally let them down . . . when in actuality all he'd done was make one bad movie, something any actor's career should be able to survive. For a while, it looked like his wouldn't.

RIGHT: *Actress Lily Tomlin.*

'My manager said to me, "I've never seen a life as accelerated as yours. For most people the good and the bad happen at a slower rate, but with you it's been boom, boom, boom!" . . . It's as if I've lived the life of a 50-year-old.'

'That was the first time I heard the words "Your career is over",' he has said on numerous occasions. 'They went beyond that fine line where criticism actually hurts, and destroys someone. I'm surprised that either Lily or I ever made a movie again after that. People who were less strong wouldn't have done.'

Moment by Moment opened December 1978 and disappeared from screens in a matter of weeks. Following the film's devastating reception, Travolta, who had finally bowed out of *Welcome Back Kotter* after four years, was left uncertain and confused, a condition exacerbated by his father's ill-health. Just one month after Helen's death, Sam had suffered a heart attack; although slowly recovering, he was not a well man.

The 1979 Golden Globe Awards must have helped soften the blows of the preceding months: Travolta was named as the Most Popular Actor in the World and admirer Fred Astaire presented him with the award. But even this event was marred when Todd Wallace, a 17-year-old photographer, claimed he had been assaulted by one of John's minders after the ceremony and promptly sued the star for $1 million.

John initially decided that, as before, concentrating on work was the best option, and so he began preparation for *American Gigolo*. The former French matinée idol Frances Lederer was giving him

'To me making a picture was always a pleasure, but then there always came the pain of releasing it. I'm talking about the stuff that goes into getting a movie out, the suspense . . . Will audiences like it? Will the critics like it? Will it earn money?'

'I know what it's like to work with big movie stars in trouble. John was so burned out by that bad film and certain tragedies in his private life. It was really bad for him.'
JAMES BRIDGES

lessons in deportment, while Giorgio Armani, at this time a relatively new name in fashion, had already outfitted him with a full wardrobe. But Travolta wasn't completely happy with the script: 'You have to be comfortable with what you're saying if the performance is to work.' The combination of events and doubts led Travolta to drop out of *American Gigolo* (although he did get to keep the Armani clothes). When the movie became a huge hit at the box office, making a star of his replacement, Richard Gere, many saw his withdrawal as yet another serious misjudgement in a career that seemed to have entered a dramatic tailspin.

Travolta entered the 1980s with a career that many had already written off, and during the decade he would give his

LEFT: *Take the hint — the movie's a dog!*

detractors plenty of evidence to support that opinion.

A mere two years after *Grease,* and with only one flop movie in between, *Urban Cowboy* (1980) was already being hailed as Travolta's 'comeback'. Travolta himself obviously felt the same way about the film. 'My success as an actor depends on this movie,' he said. 'If this one's not a hit, I'm gonna give it all up.' Based on a 1978 *Esquire* article by journalist Aaron Latham, *Urban Cowboy,* with a strong Country & Western soundtrack, offered Travolta a chance to play a more mature role: Bud Davis, an oil worker who at night takes to the floor – and the mechanical bull – of Gilley's, the world's largest honky tonk. Travolta learned such dances as the Cotton-Eyed Joe and the Whip, and it was hoped that this movie would do for the Country & Western scene what *Saturday Night Fever* had earlier done for disco. In addition to giving him a more demanding role, the movie also offered Travolta the chance to work with another established director, James Bridges. 'I hadn't really worked with a well-known director up until then, and I think it was important for the film industry to know that I could, because a lot of people were getting

---

'I tell you where I was pretty demanding – on SATURDAY NIGHT FEVER – and it paid off. The truth is I was not demanding on MOMENT BY MOMENT and you see what happened. That was my biggest lesson and I can tell you it'll never happen again.'
ON BEING 'DIFFICULT'

---

preconceived ideas I was difficult to work with,' he said.

If Travolta did have a reputation for being difficult, the filming of *Urban Cowboy* certainly added to it. Obviously feeling the pressure of needing a hit, he insisted on a completely closed set, even going as far as to bar producers Robert Evans and Irving Azoff, as well as ordering several script changes.

Urban Cowboy opened to strong reviews and good box office, with critics giving particular praise to co-star Debra Winger. 'You know what's exciting?' Travolta said with good grace, 'People are talking about the performances other than mine . . . it's time for me to share

> *'It was only after I got into showbusiness that women started to like me. Before that I wasn't popular.'*

the screen a bit.' Having torn him down, the press were quick to build Travolta back up again, claiming that 'Cowboy Fever' was sweeping the country. The film went on to make over $100 million worldwide, but its impact was certainly far less than that of either of John's first two movies.

Nevertheless, for now things were good. Wearing *Urban Cowboy* regulation Stetson and boots, John became the 162nd actor to place his hand- and shoe-prints in the cement outside Hollywood's legendary Mann's Chinese Theatre. His spot was right next to John Wayne's.

In life off the filmset John was continually active, indulging his passion for flying, co-hosting an anti-drugs television special with *Grease* co-star Olivia Newton-John, presenting an honorary Oscar to Barbara Stanwyck at the 1981 Academy Awards, and turning down up to $6.5 million — at that time the highest salary

LEFT: Urban Cowboy *proved to be a breakthrough movie for Debra Winger.*

RIGHT: *Dancing the night away at Gilley's in* Urban Cowboy.

'The role was so different for me — I've always played characters that go directly from the heart. Jack is so very analytical that it seemed like a real challenge.'
ON *BLOW OUT* (1981)

that had ever been offered to an actor — to star in the movie of the Broadway hit *A Chorus Line* (1985).

Travolta has obviously rejected many movie offers in his career, several of which later became hits — *Arthur* (1981), *Raiders of the Lost Ark* (1981) and *Splash!* (1984) among them. His critics would, with hindsight, cite these decisions as further examples of his inability to manage a career and his poor judgement, and it is true that these failings have at more than one point almost ended his career for good.

Curiously, the one person to benefit from this most has been Richard Gere. Gere shot to fame in Travolta's vacated *American Gigolo* (1980) shoes; but two years earlier he had also taken the lead in Terrence Mallick's acclaimed *Days of*

Heaven (1978) when Travolta had been forced to drop out after two weeks' rehearsal due to a scheduling conflict with *Welcome Back Kotter*. In 1982, Travolta managed the shared hat-trick by rejecting *An Officer and a Gentleman* (1982), written specifically for him by director Taylor Hackford, on the grounds that the woman's part (played by Debra Winger, hot from *Urban Cowboy*) was the better role. With Gere in his place, once again the film was a major success.

By 1981, Travolta was developing a possible script around eccentric multi-millionaire Howard Hughes' legendary folly, his *Spruce Goose* aeroplane, and approached Brian DePalma. At the time DePalma was working on a thriller called *Personal Effects*. The two agreed to swap scripts, and when Travolta read DePalma's

'I just create an effect. What happens to it when it's left me is out of my hands . . . Surely this question of appealing to both sexes is true for most actors. They almost have to if they want to make the biggest impact.'

he knew it was the role for him. Retitled *Blow Out,* the movie was a dark, complex conspiracy thriller, revolving around a movie sound technician who accidentally records an auto accident in which a leading politician dies. When he analyses the tape, the sound man realizes that what he has recorded is not in fact a tyre blowout but a gunshot, something that the mysterious powers-that-be — led by John Lithgow — cannot allow to become known.

In preparation for the role, Travolta spent three weeks working with a sound engineer, learning to handle the equipment. With a budget of $18 million, the movie was expensive; $750,000 of that sum covered the costs of restaging and reshooting the movie's central parade scene, several cans of the original film having been stolen.

'I'm so pleased with the way *Blow Out* turned out,' Travolta said on the movie's release. 'I think, for now at least, I've done my genre thriller.' *Blow Out* was Travolta's most mature and fully rounded performance to date (indeed it was the movie Quentin Tarantino later cited as his main reason for casting Travolta in *Pulp Fiction*), and the critics were quick to acknowledge it. Writing in the *New*

ABOVE: *Travolta teams up with co-star Nancy Allen and director Brian DePalma again, for the movie* Blow Out.

Yorker, Pauline Kael described Travolta as projecting 'a vibrating physical sensitivity like that of the very young Brando'.

Despite this favourable critical response the movie failed to deliver at the box office, and once again the press were quick to sound Travolta's death knell. It was inevitable that the actor could never repeat the impact of *Saturday Night Fever* and *Grease*. Together those movies had created a star and invented an iconic image of young American masculinity — tough but vulnerable, yearning but guarded. Every movie that Travolta has subsequently made has invariably been compared to these yardsticks, with anything that didn't measure up quickly being labelled a failure.

While Travolta's screen career spent most of the 1980s on a downward spiral, he was becoming a star all over again in the tabloids. In his dealings with the press over the years, Travolta has frequently shown the same distinct lack of judgement that has marred his film career, leaving himself open to criticism over his revelations about a string of women — Brooke Shields, Jane Fonda, Catherine Deneuve and Marisa Berenson among them. In some ways, this is a reflection of Travolta's peculiar naivety: he believed that if he was as honest as he was able to be with the reporter, the reporter would show him the same respect. Predictably, what the reporters showed him instead were sleazy tabloid headlines, constant innuendo and equally persistent delving into his sexual orientation.

After *Blow Out* Travolta had planned to work with DePalma again immediately on *Fire,* a biopic based on the life of

'My mother and all three of my sisters all managed to have both career and family, to have their own interests and enthusiasms. I suppose that's the way I expect women to be and, if they aren't like that, I feel there's a dimension missing. I suppose that also explains why I remain unmoved by the women's movement. The women immediately around me in my family were and are equal to the men. I know that's not true for many other women but because, as far as my deepest feelings are concerned, women are men's equals and have no problems living life exactly as they want to live it, I have great difficulty recognizing that there is a problem.'

Doors singer Jim Morrison. When the project failed to materialize, he decided to take matters into his own hands and parted ways with his manager of 12 years, Bob LeMond, signing with Mike Ovitz of Creative Artists Agency (CAA). In an attempt to turn his career around, Travolta opted to make the long-awaited *Saturday Night Fever* sequel, *Staying Alive*.

Rocky star Sylvester Stallone was lined up to direct the movie, and rapidly set about doing three things – rebuilding Travolta in the image of the body perfect, drafting in brother Frank Stallone to provide most of the movie's music, and rewriting Norman Wexler's script to the point where it became a travesty of the original.

LEFT: *Sylvester Stallone directs Travolta on everything but dress sense in* Staying Alive.

'John's legs were too thin, he was too soft and too thick around the waist. His upper body was weak, he was scrawny with no strength in his arms.'
SYLVESTER STALLONE ON A
PRE-*STAYING ALIVE* JOHN TRAVOLTA

RIGHT: *The return of Tony Manero.*

With Stallone as his personal trainer, Travolta spent 21 weeks getting in shape for his second outing as Tony Manero, lifting weights, running and learning jazz ballet dance for up to eight hours a day. 'Now I think I've got a body professional dancers would die for,' he said at the time.

Staying Alive sees Tony Manero, five years down the line, struggling to make it as a Broadway chorus dancer. He has his big break in a show described as 'a journey through Hell'; audiences and critics felt the same way about the movie, which in Stallone's hands had become a montage-heavy, leaden variation on *Rocky* in tights. *Time* summed it up best: 'Travolta is gorgeous and very charming. The rest of the film is neither.'

The movie took $12 million in its first weekend, but word of mouth quickly prevented it from becoming a blockbuster. At the time of its release,

'To me, in Staying Alive, the most important thing was my dancing. For Sly, though, it was my body.'

Travolta talked of reteaming with Sly to make a third instalment, possibly relocating Tony to Hollywood, but this never came about.

As part of the promotional push on *Staying Alive,* Travolta appeared naked but for a loincloth on the cover of *Rolling Stone* under the headline 'Sex and the Single Star'. The interview, which has haunted the actor ever since, amounted to a seriously misjudged kiss and tell, with Travolta detailing a series of relationships; many readers had known nothing about the other women in his life until they saw that issue of *Rolling Stone.* At the time Travolta naively defended himself, saying he was giving the journalist exactly what she wanted. Later, he was decidedly more honest about things: 'Why did I go that far to make an impression? I'll tell you. I'd done a thousand interviews and been on the cover of every magazine. I was just running out of things to say and do.'

In the final analysis, what was wrong with *Staying Alive* was one simple thing: in the original movie Travolta had been an amazing actor; here he was just a fit body. *Staying Alive* showed that lightning doesn't strike twice, but, demonstrating

> *'John's work is two years behind where he is as a person.'*
> MARILU HENNER

his now customary lack of judgement, Travolta needed further proof. *Two of a Kind* (1983) reteamed him with *Grease* co-star Olivia Newton-John. 'I think Olivia and I embody the fantasies of a lot of people out there,' Travolta said. 'There's a certain chemistry.' The chemistry was sorely lacking in this tale of a couple who become God's guinea pigs: in order to save the human race they must prove themselves capable of genuine goodness. 'The best thing is that we're playing against type,' Travolta said. 'For half the movie we're horrible.' Audiences and critics thought they were horrible throughout.

While flailing around in his screen career, Travolta was busy over-reaching himself in his business dealings, mounting a short-lived 'Travolta' fashion-wear line and publishing a post-*Staying Alive* fitness book. Additionally, he launched a one-to-

'The truth is I don't need another blockbuster for my career. In the list of the top-ten-grossing movies of all time, I was the only actor people came to see as an actor. The rest of the top grossers were all special effects films . . . I may be the only actor the public went to see instead of a shark.'

one personal-trainer business with fitness expert Dan Isaacson.

Before, he had always turned in moments of self-doubt to Scientology, but even this was now proving problematic for him. Founder L. Ron Hubbard had temporarily left the 'church', and 'there was this infiltration of certain personalities that disrupted the organization'. Travolta said he would return to the fold if and when Hubbard did, and was true to his word in 1985. His other main point of stability, Marilu Henner, was also missing from his life at this time, having married actor Frederic Forrest – though John and Marilu reunited when her marriage to Forrest collapsed within two years.

Travolta now had more flops to his name than hits – and some of those flops had been among Hollywood's most public. *Perfect* (1985), based on a *Rolling Stone* article by Aaron Latham (whose work had also inspired *Urban Cowboy*), proved to be his biggest mistake yet. In this movie Travolta starred, opposite Jamie Lee Curtis, as a *Rolling Stone* reporter exposing the singles scene at health clubs. 'Jim Bridges allowed me to play a cowboy when it wasn't fashionable . . . and now he's allowed me to play an intellectual, which hasn't been my image,' he said.

Travolta spent six months researching the role, going so far as to pen a number of articles on himself and his co-stars, including one that was actually published (although apparently heavily rewritten) in *Rolling Stone*.

In a curious way, the resultant film – a vapid and shallow movie that was obsessed with glorifying the bodies that its own characters were seeking to glorify themselves – was a perfect reflection of the self-obsession of the 1980s 'Me Generation'. On its release, however, it flopped dramatically.

For Hollywood, and Travolta himself, it appeared this might be the final nail in the coffin.

LEFT: *Travolta with the body perfect, Jamie Lee Curtis.*

'At first glance, you might perceive John Travolta to be, as one well known critic said, "Warren Beatty's neanderthal brother". To those that don't know him, he may appear a not particularly smart, somewhat dimwitted person. Better look again. He is really a chameleon, to the frightening degree that his empathy for people makes him become them even when he is not conscious of doing so. Even if the roles he plays call upon him to have an ability that is incongruous with his education and upbringing, he still manages to come up with the goods.'

ON HIMSELF, IN PREPARATION FOR *PERFECT*

LOOK WHO'S TALKING BACK!

'It's funny. One movie can make you and one can remake you. It's like I went to the moon, then came back down to Earth and now I can go to Mars or someplace.'

FACING PAGE: *Travolta, Kirstie Alley and the spirit of Bruce Willlis talk back to the box office!*

PRIOR TO *Perfect,* Travolta had planned to make his directorial debut on a project called *Lake Forest,* a story 'about a family that loses its wealth and has to learn to live with other values . . . It's an American tragedy that involves replacing our excessive materialism.' These plans were abandoned after the failure of *Perfect,* as Travolta went into retreat for over two years. During this time, in November 1985, he was invited to attend a formal dinner reception for the Prince and Princess of Wales at the White House, apparently at the request of Princess Diana. After dinner, he danced with her to a medley of hits from *Grease* and *Saturday Night Fever.* The event made global front-page news, with Travolta earning his best notices for years. He

---

'There was a time when I actually considered giving up acting and becoming a pilot. But you can imagine the passengers' faces when I came over the intercom and said, "This is your captain speaking, John Travolta".'

---

returned to the White House a year later with a collection of pledges from people in the entertainment industry accepting Nancy Reagan's 'Just Say No' request to help combat the use of illegal drugs.

The years following *Perfect* were a transitionary period, and at times Travolta even considered giving up acting altogether. Instead, though, he decided it was time to reassess his life and rebuild his career. First to go was agent Mike Ovitz, the man who, amongst other things, had advised him to turn down the lead in *Splash!* In his place, Travolta hired a personal manager and a lawyer, intent on overseeing deals himself. To this end he set up his own production company, MCEG Productions.

There was talk of *Saturday Night Fever 3 (Far from Over)* and of teaming with Whoopi Goldberg for a remake of Cagney's *The Public Enemy* (1931). But the one project that seemed most appealing to the actor was the lead role in Dave Clark's stage musical *Time.* Travolta was set to take over the role of the Rock Star from Cliff Richard, first in London and then on Broadway. Despite serious negotiations, Travolta eventually changed his mind.

'I think you can take risks as an artist, but don't take risks with your bank balance. Keep back whatever amount you can. Do the safe things about investing. And always sign your own cheques.'

ABOVE: *All crosswords and cockney accents — John Travolta and Tom Conti in Harold Pinter's* The Dumb Waiter.

Intent on changing his personal life as well as his career, Travolta sold his Santa Barbara ranch and bought a more modest four-bedroomed house in Spruce Creek, near Daytona Beach, Florida. The house was on 0.6 hectares (1½ acres) of land adjacent to a local country club, which extended round-the-clock service to its newest neighbour, including the use of its landing strip for his planes. The actor's only on-screen appearance during this time was on British television, when he accepted Prince Andrew's offer to take part in *It's a Royal Knockout,* a celebrity edition of the popular game show.

Looking for work that would stretch him as an actor, Travolta finally opted for Robert Altman's television adaptation of Harold Pinter's *The Dumb Waiter.* 'It's certainly no *Grease* and I was very grateful for that,' he said at the time. 'The pressure was off, that's everything in a nutshell. It was like being off-Broadway again. No stakes, no $20 million breathing down your neck.'

ABC had decided to buck programming trends and screen this serious dramatic play on network television. Travolta starred alongside Tom Conti and adopted a cockney accent for the part. Unfortunately, ABC's faith was not

'I was exhausted. It wasn't the movies, it was the publicity tours for all of them. I must have done 1400 interviews. If you had told me two years ago that I would never have to work again, I would have said "Great." A couple of years later I finally calmed down and said "I really do like being an actor and doing films." But I was worn out.'

LEFT: *Travolta, Kelly Preston and Arye Gross —* The Experts.

shared by viewers: *The Dumb Waiter* came a very disappointing 63rd in that week's ratings. Nonetheless, working with a director of Altman's calibre reawakened Travolta's desire to act again. When he returned to the big screen, however, it was as if he'd never been away: his comeback movie, *The Experts* (1988), flopped so dramatically that it was immediately withdrawn from theatres and released straight to video.

In this movie Travolta plays a nightclub manager asked to open a club in an archetypal American small town. Once in Indian Springs he discovers that he is in fact in Russia, where the KGB are using him so that they can learn American ways. In other words, *The Experts* was a weak one-joke comedy, and it once again proved Travolta was not a good judge of material.

On the personal side, however, it introduced him to Kelly Preston. Travolta was instantly attracted to his blonde co-star, although at the time she was married to actor Kevin Gage. 'When we were making *The Experts* I couldn't keep my eyes off her. She was beautiful and had an attractive inner peace.'

Much has been made of Travolta's fluctuating weight over the years, with comparisons to Marlon Brando being both inevitable and inaccurate. Travolta has always admitted a fondness for food, and as a consequence has been forced to work out to keep his figure in trim – a reported daily regime of 950 sit-ups in 12 minutes, followed by a 8km (5-mile) run. At one point, when the cast of *The Experts* had to return for additional filming months after production had wrapped, rumour was rife that Travolta had ballooned to such an alarming degree that the moviemakers would be unable to match the shots. Having caught the rumours himself, Travolta shocked director Dave Thomas by appearing on set wearing a fat body-suit.

He followed *The Experts* with what remains his least seen movie appearance, *The Tender* (1989), the sentimental tale of a dog adopted by the family of a recovering alcoholic (Travolta). While filming in Vancouver, he met up again with Kelly

'I don't feel like a victim, never have. I don't blame anybody for anything in my life. I don't like blame, shame or regret.'

'John is snatching at B-movie scripts he would once have shredded.'
JERRY WURMS, ONE-TIME HEAD OF JOHN'S PRODUCTION COMPANY

Preston. In the intervening months, Preston had separated from her husband and been briefly engaged to actor Charlie Sheen. Now she was single, and Kelly and John fell in love.

Before he was to walk Preston down a Scientology-assisted aisle, Travolta decided to make a movie about a talking baby. Everybody thought it was a bad idea: Travolta would play a slightly chubby cab driver who falls for single mother Kirstie Alley, whose son Mikey would be voiced 'hilariously' by Bruce Willis. 'I loved the part because it let me be more mature. I am 36 and I could play myself, and I could play it as an overweight character. It was great to be fat.' However, the movie company, Columbia TriStar, didn't initially share Travolta's enthusiasm, deeming writer-director Amy Heckerling's final efforts to be all but

'We were both wary of committing too quickly. Just a few months after I promised not to rush things, I asked Kelly to marry me. Luckily, she said yes.'
ON WIFE-TO-BE KELLY PRESTON

unreleasable. But Travolta had a feeling about it: he *knew* it would be a hit. And, when the test scores began coming back from preview audiences, he was for once proved right. Columbia TriStar released *Look Who's Talking* (1989) nationwide, and the movie went on to make $135 million in America alone. Travolta, once again, was back.

While he may not always have made the right moves on screen, to say the least, Travolta has proved to be an astute businessman, leaving him more than able to live up to his oft-quoted description of a 'millionaire who lives like a billionaire'.

On *Look Who's Talking* he had wisely opted to take a percentage of the profits, thus adding considerably to his large personal fortune.

Certainly not for the first (or last) time in his career, the media latched on to the idea of the 'Travolta comeback'. *Look Who's Talking* put him back on magazine covers worldwide, and people seemed glad to have him there again. But, in typical Travolta style, he almost blew it again.

Chains of Gold (1990) was a personal project that Travolta had developed through his MCEG company. Based on real-life events, this movie portrayed Travolta as a social worker desperately trying to save a young boy from a gang of crack cocaine dealers. For the first time Travolta took a co-writing credit on the screenplay. It was a sincere movie, one of the first to confront the difficult issue of crack, and it featured a fine, impassioned performance from the actor. However, it was yet another flop – as was *Shout!* (1991), an uninspired drama with Travolta's rebel teacher bringing rock'n'roll to the repressed children of an American small town in the mid-1950s.

Almost as soon as it had begun the great comeback seemed to be over, with not even the box office success of *Look's Who's Talking Too!* (1990) – which had the voices of Roseanne Barr and Damon Wayans thrown into the mix – proving strong enough to dispel the image of Travolta as a has-been, forced into playing second banana to a voice-over.

The actor's private life was problematical, too. In 1990 a porn-movie actor,

'Princess Di wanted to dance with me and I thought to myself, even when things are bad, they're pretty damned good.'

'In 1975 I became big and it took me until 1985 to learn how to deal with it.'

LEFT: *Travolta acts opposite old flame Marilu Henner in* Chains of Gold.

Paul Baressi, claimed to have had a two-year homosexual affair with Travolta. Shortly after, in May 1991, a cover story in *Time* magazine slammed the Church of Scientology. In passing, the article stated: 'High-level defectors claim Travolta has long feared, if he defected, details of his sex life would be made public.' Richard Aznarian, the church's former head of security, reported that he had heard the current leader David Miscaviage joking with staff about

'After I had been the only actor in town for eight years there was an onslaught of wonderful actors that came on the scene. Tom Hanks, Kevin Costner, Michael Keaton, Tom Cruise . . . but I'd rather be part of a group than the only one. You had no competition, you had no one to compare yourself to. It was boring, to be honest.'

'Travolta's alleged promiscuous homosexual behaviour'.

Travolta remained silent about all these events; the one thing he was prepared to tell the world was that, on New Year's Eve, he had asked Kelly Preston to marry him, and she had said yes. The couple were wed on September 6, 1991, in a secret ceremony held at the luxurious Crillon Hotel, Paris; the service was conducted by a minister from the Church of Scientology (Preston was a convert). For legal reasons the ceremony was then repeated in America the following week. Travolta bought a 20-bedroom mansion in Maine as a suitable home for his new bride.

At the time that the ceremony took place Kelly Preston was pregnant; their son, named Jett on account of Travolta's love of flying, was born on April 13 of the following year, weighing in at 4kg (8lb 12oz).

While his personal life had now, so swiftly, recovered to an all-time high, Travolta's career, which admittedly had had far more than its fair share of ups and downs, was paradoxically heading for an all-time low. Even a mineral-water advertisement that he had made for

'I'm shy. Does that surprise anyone? I think it has always been rather obvious. I found out a few years ago that I will always be shy. People have often asked what the real John Travolta is like. I still don't know myself. I only know I like to act and dance and entertain.'

'If I am androgynous, I'd say I lean towards the macho androgynous.'

Italian television couldn't find an audience when the government banned it; in the advertisement Travolta stated that Italy had as many mineral-water companies as it did political parties, and then advised viewers to 'choose well'. Coming as it did just a matter of days before a general election was to be held, the advertisement was abruptly withdrawn as being 'political'.

Attending a party thrown to mark the 20th anniversary of the musical *Grease,* Travolta met up again with Olivia Newton-John, briefly sparking rumours of a possible *Grease 3,* which would focus on Danny and Sandy in modern times with kids of their own. However, the movie Travolta chose to make instead was *Look Who's Talking Now!,* in which the talking babies were replaced by talking dogs. 'That was a movie I was doing to stay alive in show business,' was his explanation.

'On a daily level with business, family and friends, there's nothing you can't apply it to. It's almost fun. If I can't figure something out, I can look it up in my Scientology book. It's like a handbook for the mind.'

THE COMEBACK KING

'Right before I was offered PULP FICTION,
I started to lose confidence in my career.
Not in my talents, but in my career.
I was thinking, "Maybe it's all over, maybe
I have to face the fact that for whatever
reason, this doesn't work as far as film is
concerned any more."'

FACING PAGE: 'A "please" would be nice.' Hitmen Vincent Vega and Jules Winfield, Pulp Fiction.

IN 1992, former video-store worker Quentin Tarantino made his first movie, a gritty, violent look at the aftermath of a heist gone awry. *Reservoir Dogs* became an instant critical smash, giving its young director a shot at doing just about anything he liked as a follow-up. While travelling round Europe to promote *Reservoir Dogs,* Tarantino began to

LEFT: Pulp Fiction *director Quentin Tarantino.*

write a screenplay called *Pulp Fiction,* a collection of three overlapping stories, drawing together such diverse elements as the cheap crime novels that inspired the title and his recent pan-European cultural experiences, such as the fact that you can buy a beer in a movie theatre and how in McDonald's in Paris a quarterpounder is called a Royale.

The script that emerged had one character who loosely linked the three separate tales. Vincent Vega was a hitman-heroin addict, and Tarantino wanted John Travolta for the role. One of the permanent fixtures on Tarantino's constantly evolving list of Top Ten movies was *Blow Out*, and he had always felt that Travolta had never really fulfilled the promise he had shown in this and his other early movies. 'Much as I like John Travolta,' he told *Vanity Fair,* 'I couldn't bring myself to watch some fuckin' talking-baby movie. But I've seen everything else he's done and he's one of my favourite actors.'

Having just finished *Look Who's Talking Now!,* Travolta was — it is fair to say — not optimistic about his career. So, when the hottest young director in town called and asked for a meeting, John was interested enough to go along to Tarantino's

ABOVE: *Travolta,
Uma Thurman,
Quentin Tarantino and
Bruce Willis, Cannes,
1994*

Tarantino told Travolta about the movie and, although he was uncertain if the hitman role was right for him, John listened eagerly.

Six months later the script for *Pulp Fiction* arrived at Travolta's home. Following their meeting, Tarantino had written the role of Vincent Vega specifically for Travolta, the name Vincent

apartment. Both men must have taken it as a good omen when Travolta arrived on Tarantino's doorstep and discovered that this was the very same apartment Travolta had rented when he had first moved out to Los Angeles nearly 20 years before. What should have been just a short business meeting turned into a 12-hour session during which Travolta indulged Tarantino's peculiar passion for playing movie-related board games with members of their original cast — the latter had the *Welcome Back Kotter*, *Saturday Night Fever* and *Grease* games in his collection.

'He said "What did you do? Don't you remember what Pauline Kael said about you? What Truffaut said about you? What Bertolucci said about you? Don't you know what you mean to American cinema? John, what did you do?" I was hurt — but moved. He was telling me I'd had a promise like no one else's. I was devastated but I also thought, "Jesus Christ, I must have been a fucking good actor."*

ON HIS FIRST MEETING WITH
QUENTIN TARANTINO

FROM THE CREATOR OF
RESERVOIR DOGS

THE HITMAN

"You play with matches, you get burned."

WINNER BEST FILM

JOHN TRAVOLTA

PULP FICTION

A FILM BY QUENTIN TARANTINO

18

'I want to show that I can do more than play safe, pretty-boy roles. This movie has it all. I've been waiting a long time for a role like this.'

ON VINCENT VEGA

being chosen in partial reference to Vinnie Barbarino. The actor was hugely impressed but still had reservations. 'I read the movie and I thought, "Wow, it's really good, but is it too violent, too much for me?"'

Initially Tarantino had difficulty persuading the movie's financiers Miramax that Travolta was right for the lead, the studio feeling that his time had really come and gone. But the director stood by his choice and eventually Travolta was cast as Vincent Vega. Despite an all-star cast that included Bruce Willis, Samuel L. Jackson, Uma Thurman and Rosanna Arquette, *Pulp Fiction* was made for a relatively modest $8 million, with Travolta taking a basic fee of $100,000. Paying for better hotel accommodation than the production allowed and having his wife and son with him while filming actually left Travolta out of pocket to the tune of an additional $30,000. 'I felt the same way about doing *The Dumb Waiter* with Robert Altman. These are the movies you make to keep your integrity as an artist. And also to know why you're doing the stupid ones.'

Pulp Fiction (1994) gave Travolta his best role since *Saturday Night Fever,* and the actor leapt at the opportunity.

'*I said either this is going to be the best move of my career or the worst because I have never seen an actor on the toilet, especially someone who's supposedly a superstar.*'
ON *PULP FICTION*

'Quentin allowed me to do what I wanted with it. Because the hair, the earring, the way I talked, the way I walked . . . the take I had on it was very eccentric.' *Pulp Fiction* received its world premiere in competition at the 1994 Cannes Film Festival. The judges, headed by Clint Eastwood, awarded the movie the top honour of the Palme d'Or, with Travolta, Thurman, Jackson and Willis accompanying Tarantino on stage to collect the award. The movie went on to become a worldwide phenomenon, moving far beyond the cult adulation of *Reservoir Dogs,* eventually grossing over $100 million in America alone. Throughout all the attendant hype Travolta was singled out for praise. Once again the talk was of comebacks, but this time it was for real. *Pulp Fiction* had

undone years of talking-baby damage and reawakened people to just how good an actor John Travolta could really be. Tarantino had sought to reinvent one of his heroes and, when in early 1995 Travolta received the second Academy Award nomination of his career, it was clear he had more than pulled it off.

Sixteen years after it had first featured him on the cover, *Time* ran a profile of Travolta headlined 'Travolta Fever'. John Travolta had been rediscovered by a Hollywood that was only too glad to find him. After all the comeback talk, he

'*I think a generation denied loving me, meaning they secretly loved me but were afraid to admit it . . . Even Harvey Keitel said to me, "My favourite movie's* GREASE *and you got me out of a depression, I would watch* KOTTER *every week because it would make me happy." That's so wonderful that somebody can now admit it.*'

'It was last year's story and prior to that it was a story in '89 and prior to that it was a story in '83, and prior to that it was a story in '80. I've never quite figured out why I'm the comeback kid when another actor might just have a normal career of movies that work and don't work.'

looked like he was here again for good. And fame the second time around took many forms — film critic Gene Siskel auctioned off Travolta's white polyester suit from *Saturday Night Fever,* raising a record $145,500, American art-house cinemas began screening that movie and *Grease* to packed audiences, and punk band Extra Fancy put out their single 'You Look Like A Movie Star' in a sleeve that featured Travolta in his classic *Fever* pose, sans clothing; Travolta sued to withhold the release, but by then the record had sold out.

Shortly after *Pulp Fiction* was released in America, Travolta discussed his career with actress Rosanna Arquette in *Interview* magazine, recalling his experience of stardom the first time around. 'I was very alone in those days,' he reflected. 'In a way I created several themes for people to party on — *Saturday Night Fever, Grease, Urban Cowboy* — and people partied on those themes in a way that I never did.' He also discussed his relationship with Scientology. 'I was not into drugs, nor was I a drinker. But that was because I was studying Scientology. You see, in order to do certain courses you had to be straight because it was illegal within the group to be high. And I liked the result of that better than I did being high.'

Actors live insecure lives, knowing full well that at any point what a producer or an audience thinks about them can turn them from gold-dust into just plain dust; their worth is measured by demand.

'I've walked down the street with some big stars, okay? I cannot walk two feet with John Travolta. People are clawing all over him.'
QUENTIN TARANTINO

Very few of them have ever experienced what it was like to be in John Travolta's shoes the first time around; no one in Hollywood history has ever experienced it on this scale for a second time. Travolta himself, who appeared genuinely humbled by *Pulp Fiction's* reception, said it best when he stood on that stage at Cannes, as Tarantino accepted the Palme d'Or for the movie: 'I felt not only that the film was being celebrated but that I was being celebrated.'

Travolta was a modern superstar before Hollywood knew how to deal with modern superstars. While others managed successful careers, Travolta floundered with talking dogs; it was clearly a mistake and one he seems determined not to repeat.

Quentin Tarantino has become a potent voice, guiding the career he helped to resurrect. Travolta's first post-*Pulp Fiction* movie was *White Man's Burden* (1995), an inverted racism drama for *Pulp Fiction* producer Lawrence Bender. In a society in which blacks are the dominant race, Travolta played an aggrieved working-class white man who kidnaps Harry Belafonte. 'Like *Pulp Fiction*, when I read it, without exaggeration, I couldn't

'I don't think there's ever been anyone who's genuinely loved me more than Quentin. He doesn't want anything back, other than my well-being, and every time I think about the purity of that it makes me want to cry. And Steven Spielberg. So with Quentin Tarantino and Steven Spielberg, I think I have the best guardian angels the planet has to offer.'

RIGHT: *Dancing the night away at Jack Rabbit Slim's — Travolta with Uma Thurman in* Pulp Fiction.

'Oppression, regardless of the details, is not OK. It [WHITE MAN'S BURDEN] is an uncomfortable movie to watch. It can be irritating. But so is SCHINDLER'S LIST, you know?'

put it down. I stood in my bathroom and read it until it was finished. I knew it wasn't commercial, but I thought, "I know how to play this guy to the hilt. I should do this."'

Before *White Man's Burden* was released, however, Travolta confirmed his renewed box-office stature with *Get Shorty* (1995). Spurred on by Tarantino's advice, he took the lead role of Elmore Leonard's Chili Palmer, a loan shark who finds his feet in the movie business, in this delicious send-up of Hollywood. Travolta picked up $5 million for the role, and when the movie proved to be a hit his asking price went through the roof.

He has followed *Get Shorty* with *Broken Arrow* (1996), an action movie for Hong Kong filmmaker John Woo, once again on the advice of Quentin Tarantino, a long-time Woo advocate. The movie offered Travolta his first big-screen stab at a villain (if one ignores his teen-nasty part in *Carrie*), playing a stealth bomber pilot opposite Christian Slater's hero.

Wisely opting to strike while the iron was hot, Travolta next filmed the fantasy *Phenomenon* (1996), playing the role of a man who turns into a genius when struck by lightning. This was followed by *Michael* (1996), Nora Ephron's comedic

LEFT: Travolta with Christian Slater in Broken Arrow.

'Quentin said, "This is not the one you say no to. This is the one you say yes to. I'm not going to let you make this mistake".'
ON REJECTING *GET SHORTY* TWICE

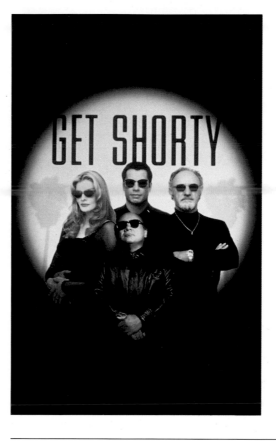

tale of a booze-hound angel alive and well and living in Iowa. In what has transpired to be the most active phase of his career to date, Travolta has since signed to play not one but two Americans in Paris for exiled director Roman Polanski; for this movie, *The Double,* Travolta got a reported fee of $17 million.

On the strength of *Pulp Fiction* and the box-office performance of both *Get Shorty* and *Broken Arrow*, John Travolta gave full and final notice that he knew how to play the Hollywood game, exceeding the previous record payment for an actor by a single dollar, signing a three-picture deal for $20,000,001 per picture. In an age of inflated egos, inflated salaries and inflated budgets, John Travolta, the only star that the movies have genuinely made twice, had thus become the highest-paid actor in history. And he can still dance.

'Look, the worst that can happen is that they all fail, right? And if they do, who better to make a comeback than me?'

FILMOGRAPHY

Carrie, *1976.* **The Boy in the Plastic Bubble** *(television movie), 1976.*
Saturday Night Fever *(Academy Award Nomination Best Actor), 1977.*
Grease *1978.* **Moment by Moment,** *1978.* **Urban Cowboy,** *1980.*
Blow Out, *1981.* **Staying Alive,** *1983.* **Two of a Kind,** *1983.*
Perfect, *1985.* **The Dumb Waiter** *(television movie), 1986*
The Experts, *1986.* **The Tender,** *1989.* **Look Who's Talking,** *1989.*
Chains of Gold, *1990.* **Look Who's Talking Too!,** *1990.*
Shout!, *1991.* **Look Who's Talking Now!,** *1993.*
Pulp Fiction *(Academy Award Nomination, Best Actor), 1994.*
White Man's Burden, *1995.* **Get Shorty,** *1995.*
Broken Arrow, *1996.* **Phenomenon,** *1996.* **Michael,** *1996.*